Grow Where You Are Planted

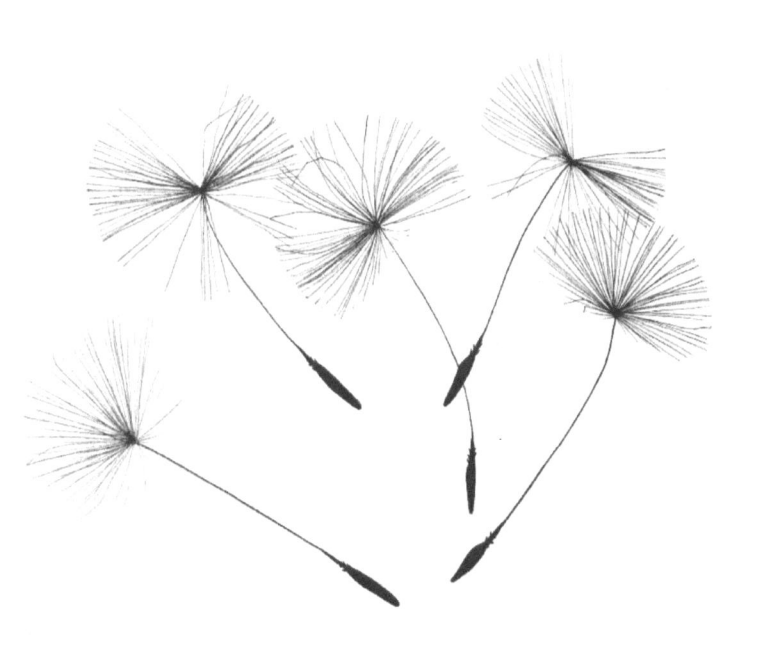

Laura Patton

Grow Where You Are Planted ©

Copyright Laura Patton 2020

Scripture taken from the International Children's Bible®. Copyright © 1986, 1988, 1999 by Thomas Nelson, Inc. Used by permission. All rights reserved.

Title Font and Heading Font: JeanSunHo This freeware font is the property of Kevin Richey. © 2008. All rights reserved.

Dedication

This devotional is dedicated to my children, Emma and Sam, who continuously show me how to be resilient to change in this military life. Also, to all of the military children around the world who are strong, supportive, and compassionate. They may be children of service members in the US, but they are also members in God's army!

A word to military kids from military kids:

It's fine to be scared and miss your friends, but you can see your friends again. You might have to move a lot, or your parent might have to leave, but pray that they will be safe and that no weapon formed against them or us shall prosper. Even though being a military kid is scary, you will get to see things others can't see. You are going to do great and you will succeed as a military kid!

-Emma Patton-

The fun things about being a military kid are you get to move around a lot, you can make new friends, and you get to live on a military base. One thing you also get to do is help the new military students at school. I like that you get to learn about new stuff at your new school. You are going to have so much fun as a military kid!

-Samuel Patton-

Day 1

Starting A New Day

Psalm 118: 24 This is the day that the Lord has made. Let us rejoice in it!

Did you know that God has created today for you to use your abilities and to fulfill your purpose that He has created you for?

Today is a day to be conquered and for you to create it with wonderful memories. God created today for new things to begin and old things to be in the past. Even though God made today, you might face hard times in your day but since God created the day, He knows what is going to happen already. Since God knows the end from the beginning, you can trust that He is already in your day ready to help you and guide you. With knowing that God is in your day and has created it, put your trust in Him and be confident in knowing that you have the one true God on your side!

So, whatever your day may bring always remember to REJOICE!!!!!

Prayer:

Lord, I pray that You help me in my day and that You guide me with Your gentle hand. I pray that You will use me throughout my day to show others Your love and who You are in my life. Protect my family, friends, and me so that we all may have a day full of Your favor. Amen!

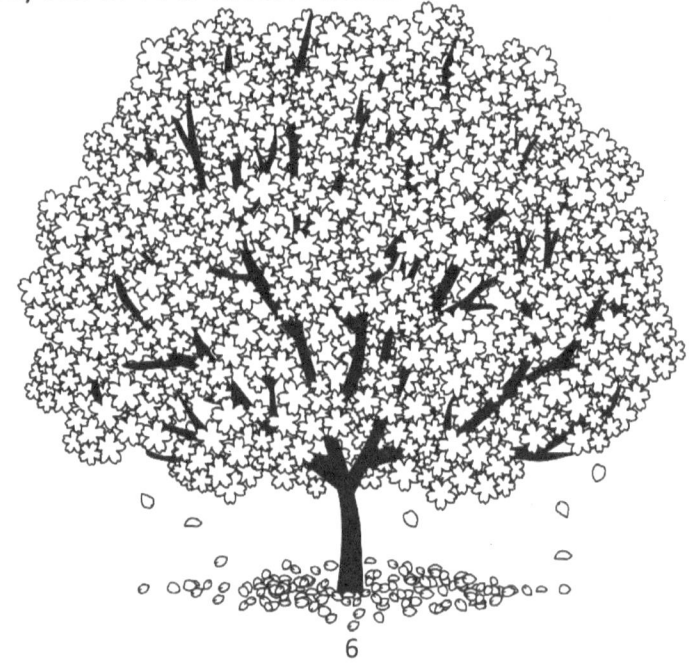

Day 2

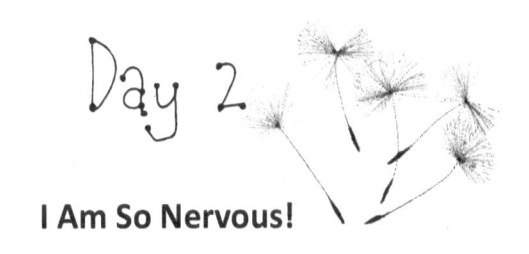

I Am So Nervous!

Philippians 4:6 Do not worry about anything. But pray and ask God for everything you need. And when you pray, always give thanks.

Have you ever felt nervous about moving to a new home or to a new school? Well, guess what? That is very normal and everyone, even your mom and dad, get nervous from time-to-time about new things.

Being a military kid brings many new challenges and changes that can be a little scary since you have to find new friends, a new home, a new church, and a new life altogether. One thing God tells us to do in His Word is to not be scared or nervous but to praise Him for the new things that He is doing for us. Praise Him that you get to see new parts of the world and experience new cultures that only some can dream of. The best part about the new things is that the God who lives in your heart is never changing and is always the same, so trust Him and know that He knows right where you are and what you need to grow in your new place!

Prayer:

Lord, I pray today that You fill my heart with Your peace and patience during this new place in my life. I pray that You lead my family and me to the places You have set aside for us and that You make it known in our lives that this is where we are supposed to be doing life at in this time. Amen!

Day 3

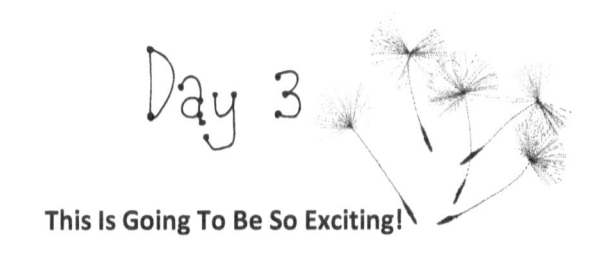

This Is Going To Be So Exciting!

Psalm 144:15 Happy are those who are like this. Happy are the people whose God is the Lord.

Excitement is such a fun feeling and it is one of those emotions that you want to always be in. Excitement happens because we look forward to something we want and can't wait to do!

God gives us excitement because it gives us the energy to get things done to get where we need to be. When you get ready to move to a new place there is so much excitement because you know that you will get to see new things and might even end up seeing your old friends from your last home. You might even get to finally live in a place with snow which you might have never seen, or get to live near a beautiful beach that you will get to go to all the time! God wants us to be excited! Don't hold back your excitement, but praise God for the opportunity that is coming your way and get to packing!

Prayer:

Father God, today, let my heart's prayer be that I always embrace the excitement of the things You have prepared for me. I know there will be days that will not be so exciting, but I pray that I will have more exciting days that outweigh the bad. Amen!

Day 4

I Am Feeling So Lonely And Sad

Deuteronomy 31:6 Be strong and brave. Don't be afraid of them. Don't be frightened. The Lord your God will go with you. He will not leave you or forget you.

Feeling lonely and being sad almost always go together because many things can cause us to be alone which makes us not happy since no one is around to cheer us up.

When you move away from a place you have called home for so long and you get to a new place, this is one of those times that you will feel lonely. The good thing about this feeling is that it will pass as you grow in your new surroundings and make new friends, or even get into a new routine. God calls us to be brave and strong, even on the days where we feel that we are the saddest, because God has it all under control. He is with you in your new house, at your new school, at your new church, and even when you are asleep. He promises to never leave us or forget us which is why we should never feel lonely.

God is always our Best Friend!

Prayer:

Lord God, I ask that You remind me daily that You are with me so that I may not feel alone and sad in this new place. In my quiet times, I pray that You speak to me and comfort me so that I know You are always in control. Amen!

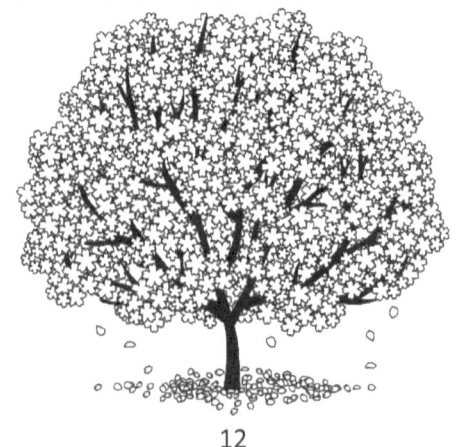

Day 5

It Is Time To Make New Friends

1 Corinthians 15:33 Do not be fooled: "Bad friends will ruin good habits."

Having a lot of friends is always a great thing, but be careful who you choose to be your friends because not everyone is meant to be our friend.

When moving to a new place, you might get so eager to find a friend that you might just choose anyone to be friends with. This is not a good way to make friends since there are some people that might lead us down a wrong way. As a Child of God, we are meant to follow the ways He calls us to so that things will go good for us, but if we connect with the wrong friends, it can lead us to trouble. Let God lead you to those friends that He wants for you because He knows those who will take care of you and you will take care of them as well.

Find friends that encourage you, but at the same time, be a friend who encourages as well, because it is about the quality of a friendship and not the number of friends.

Prayer:

Lord, I pray that You bring to me the friend You have called to be in my life. I know that there will be many people who come into my life who say they are my friends, but help me to know who should stay and who should not. I pray for friends who will be a blessing and that I may be a blessing to others. Amen.

Day 6

Feeling Homesick?

Isaiah 66:13 I will comfort you as a mother comforts her child. You will be comforted in Jerusalem.

Give yourself a second to think about how you felt when your mom or dad comforted you when you were sad. How did it make you feel when they comforted you? I bet it made you feel so much better.

There are going to be times that your house does not feel like a home for very many reasons, and you can be homesick not just for missing your house. Your house might not feel like a home because it's a new place, or there might be feelings of anger about moving, or just because you are not comfortable in the new home yet. God wants us to call on Him for comfort in the times when we just miss our "home" and we need a place to run to. God is our strong tower and, if we lean on Him, then we will see that He will change that house into a home that is comfortable and safe for us.

Prayer:

Lord, I pray that You make my house a home and that everyone who comes into my house will feel Your presence in it. I invite You into my home and every room that is in it so that it will be a place of safety and love. Amen.

Day 7

A Welcoming Home

Matthew 10:12 When you enter that home, say, "Peace be with you."

Imagine if a home could talk and when you walk up to the house, it says, "Welcome, I'm glad to see you!"

That would be a crazy thing to see, but did you know that you can talk to a house, or even pray over a house that would love to welcome you if it could talk? Every time we move to a new house, our family prays over every wall, doorway, and the outside. The reason is because we are anointing our home with prayer that we will live and feel peace every time we walk in, no matter what we face that day. When the military tells us, it is time to move again we pray over that house for the new people who move in so they will feel the same peace we had in that house. Pray for your house because it can definitely welcome you with peace.

Prayer:

Father God, as I enter a new home with new beginnings, I pray over this home that it will be filled with joy in times of sorrow, happiness in times of anger, and safety when I feel scared. My home will be a home of victory and full of your presence so that we may be victorious in all things. Amen.

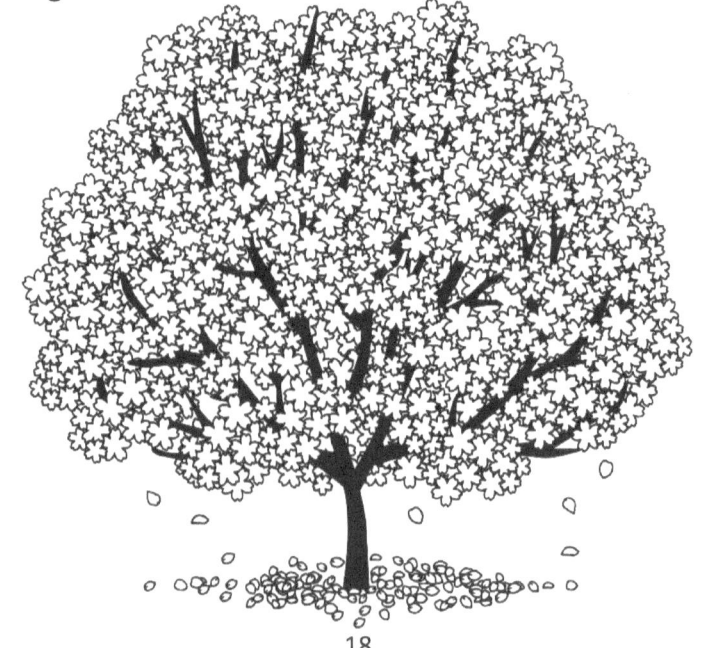

Day 8

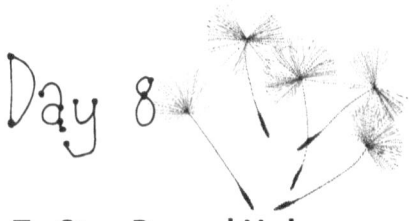

You Have To Stay Prayed Up!

Jeremiah 33:3 Pray to me, and I will answer you. I will tell you important secrets. You have never heard these things before.

No one, and I mean no one, can pray to God or have a relationship with God for you. This is very important because people can pray for you, but it is up to you to believe in that prayer.

Some of the greatest things about God is He is always there, always awake, and always ready to listen. Another of the many great things about God is that no prayer that we pray is too big or too small for God to take interest in. He wants us to talk to Him, not because He doesn't know what is going on, because He does, but He wants us to tell Him our hearts. We have to stay in constant communication with Him because He can let us know about things that we don't know about and He can help us avoid going in a wrong direction. Tell God about your day and, if you have a problem, ask Him to help you and to let you know how you should handle your problem.

Prayer:

Lord, I pray that I always hear Your voice letting me know that You are near to me. I want to stay in communication with You so that I develop a deeper relationship and love with You. I pray that I find myself so deep in You that no one can change the way I follow You. Amen.

Day 9

Don't Let Anger Set In

Proverbs 15:1 A gentle answer turns away wrath, but a harsh word stirs up anger.

It should not come as a surprise to anyone that there will be days that you will be angry. Sometimes people or situations will make you just plain angry.

As Christians, some people may think that we never get angry, or that we never get to the point of frustration. I'm here to tell you that it is natural to be angry or frustrated at times, but what comes out of our mouths during those times should be carefully spoken. If we get in an argument with our friends or family, the words we should speak are words of life. You can either build someone up or tear someone down with words and, when we are angry, that is when we really need for God to speak through us. Being angry is only for a short time but if harsh words are spoken then those hurt feelings can last a long time. So be careful what you say and who you say it to so that in the end God may get the glory and you will be able to keep those relationships that mean so much to you.

Prayer:

Father, I pray that You help me control my tongue in the times I am the angriest or most frustrated. I only want to speak Your words so please fill my mouth with what You want me to say so that You will be glorified. Amen.

Day 10

Learning To Go With The Flow

Romans 8:28 We know that in everything God works for the good of those who love him. They are the people God called, because that was his plan.

As a military kid, you might have or will experience, a time when you or your family will not be able to make plans. This comes with the territory of being a military family and as much as it is not fun, you have to go with it.

Not knowing how long you might live somewhere can be a tough part of being a military kid because you can't plan what you will do in a year or so. There are some jobs in the military that you stay longer and some that the families move every couple of years. One thing to remember is that things will change even when we don't want them to, but God has a plan for us. Make a calendar and go week to week instead of month-to-month or year-to-year. Celebrate the times you have been able to fulfill those plans and see how to fulfill those plans in your new place in case you couldn't in your last home. Your parent may have to leave quickly and, as sad as it is, make the most out of every moment you have with them, so you can have those memories to hold you over until they get back home.

Prayer:

Father, I know that my timing is not Yours and You know the plans You have for me. I pray that I will be able to adapt to the changes of the military life and that not only will I succeed in my role as a military kid, but I will excel at it! I trust in You, Lord, with all the plans You have for my life, even when I want to do something else, because I know You have great things in store for me! Amen.

Day 11

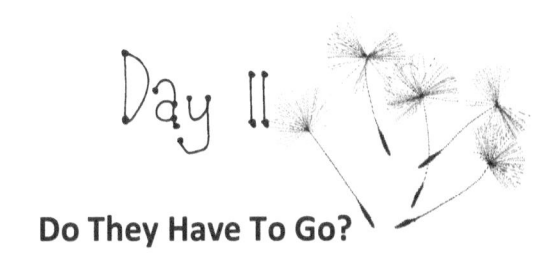

Do They Have To Go?

Genesis 31:49 …. Let the Lord watch over us while we are separated from each other.

Have you had to say goodbye to your mom or dad at the airport, or on the base when they are getting ready to leave for a long time? This is probably one of the hardest things to do as a military kid, to be honest.

When your mom or dad has to leave, whether for a year or for a couple of weeks, it can be very hard to say 'goodbye' and to be without them for some time. There will be times when they cannot be there to attend special events or activities that you are involved. The one thing that makes it a little easier is that God watches over you, your family members, and the family member who is having to leave. God keeps an eye out to make sure that the family stays together, even when they are apart, and one thing you can do to help is to send letters, care packages, or just a video phone call to say 'hi'. Those little things that we can do go a long way and help make the time apart a little easier, and makes it go by a little faster.

Prayer:

Father, I pray that You watch over my family and me while we are apart from mom / dad. Help the time that we are far from each other go smoothly and quickly so that we can be back together soon. I know that this is in Your plan for our lives, so I will embrace it, and I will grow from this experience. Amen.

Day 12

Do I Have To Go?

2 Thessalonians 3:16 We pray that the Lord of peace will give you peace at all times and in every way. May the Lord be with all of you.

'Goodbyes' are always hard and, honestly, will never get easier, but, as you grow older, you will realize that those friendships that are the hardest to say 'bye' to are the greatest.

Just when you are comfortable, and everything is going the way you want, you are told you have to move. When it comes time to say that 'goodbye' to your friend before you leave, you want to just stay in that moment forever. What a blessing! How can I say a good thing about a sad situation? That means that you have friends to say 'bye' to and that it is just as hard for them to say 'bye' to you as it is for you to say 'bye' to them. God creates us to be a blessing to others and, if we follow His rules and His guidelines, then we will meet those friends that will be the hardest to say bye to. Good thing is that you can write to them, call them, visit them, or even video chat with them. If you don't like 'goodbyes', then it's a 'see ya later!'

Prayer:

Lord, I ask that You help me and my friends to say 'goodbye' when it comes time but to cherish the memories that we have made so far. I know that it will be hard, but You give us peace in knowing that we are part of the body of Christ and, one day, we can connect together again. Amen.

Day 13

Don't Overdo It!

Galatians 6:5 Each person must be responsible for himself.

It often happens that the oldest child of the family usually takes on roles and responsibilities when only one parent is around and the other is gone. This is usually more of a hurtful thing than it is a helpful one when it comes to your childhood.

God expects for us to help and respect our parents, but what God does not want is for you to take on more responsibility than you are ready for. It is normal to feel the need to have to help your mom or dad a little more when the other parent is gone and that is a great thing! Whenever and wherever you can help, I say go for it. At the end of the day, though, you are still a child and need to have playtime and rest time. You have responsibilities such as homework and chores that are already expected of you, so focus on your original responsibilities and, when you have extra time, dedicate that time to helping your parent where you can. God will reward you for being obedient.

Prayer:

Lord, I ask that You help me put my responsibilities in order so that I may get my stuff done but also that I can lend a helping hand. I pray that You give my parents strength to do what they have to do and that You give me strength to help out as well. Amen.

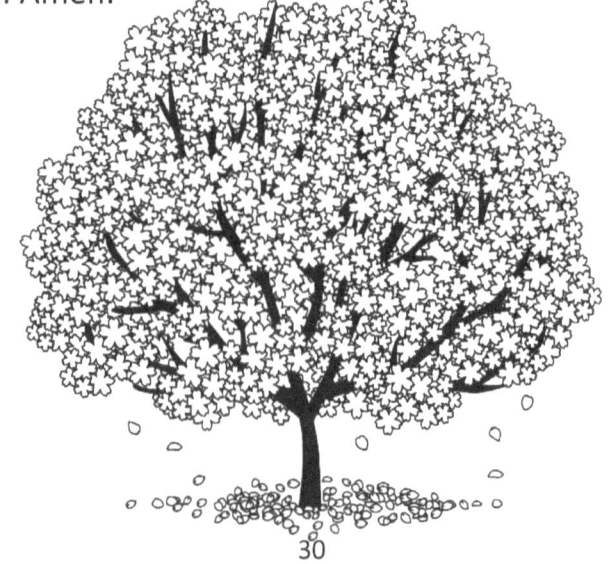

Day 14

What To Do About Long Distance Relationships

Matthew 18:19 Also, I tell you that if two of you on earth agree about something, then you can pray for it. And the thing you ask for will be done for you by my Father in heaven.

Do you have a pen and paper? Good! Do you have a phone? Good! These are tools you can use to keep in contact with family and friends, near and far.

God tells us that when two of us on earth agree about something, pray! One of the best ways to keep a relationship going whether it is with your cousins, parent, grandparent, or friends far away is to pray with another that your relationship will be strengthened. Before you move away, get your friends' and families' mailing addresses so you can send them postcards from your new home, or letters telling them of all your wonderful adventures. Use your phone to call them to just say 'hello'. As long as you pay attention to your relationships, they will never fade away, but they will continue to grow and won't be broken, no matter the distance.

Prayer:

Lord, I pray that You help me maintain the true integrity of my relationships while we are apart from each other. Give me wisdom on how to communicate and when to communicate so that I never lose sight of those friendships that You gave me. Amen.

Day 15

I Don't Know How I Can Be Without You

Proverbs 18:10 The Lord is like a strong tower. Those who do what is right can run to him for safety.

Think of a time when your mom and dad left you somewhere and you became anxious about being left alone. Thoughts running through your head of, "Are they going to come back for me? Are they ok without me?"

When your mom or dad has to leave again for a long period of time, you may start to feel the nervous bug in your tummy wiggle around. What will happen to them while they are gone? Will they be back? When are they going to be back? We all have or had this feeling at some time and, in those times of being anxious, God calls us to lean on Him and rest because He is our strength. He is taking care of our family member who is away, and He is taking care of you, so when you feel that anxious bug, know that God is there to hold you. He is there to comfort and to love you so that you know you are not alone and that He is there to make sure that nothing can harm you or your family.

Prayer:

Father God, I pray that You give me peace so that I may not feel anxious about the circumstances that I will deal with while my parent is away. I know that You are guiding us, and You know all things before we do, so I pray that You hold me in the times I feel the most scared and worried. Amen.

Day 16

No One Is Better Than The Other

Galatians 1:10 Do you think I am trying to make people accept me? No! God is the One I am trying to please.

Have you ever had someone think they are better than you just because of who their parent is, or maybe because they have better grades than you?

Guess what? Neither one of those things matter when it comes to Jesus Christ and how He feels about us. God's desire is that we please Him first and that all others come afterwards, because it is through Him that we find favor with everyone else. If you look to always please the people of this world, you will never win, because it is for a short time, but God's favor is eternal. If we put God first, we will always win since He is always fighting our battles. It does not matter what others think of what you are doing, if God calls you to do it, then obey Him and watch Him make you stand out above the rest.

Prayer:

Father, I pray that I never lose sight of pleasing You and You alone. You are my first love and the one who knows me the best so, therefore, I want You to be number one in my life. I want to respect others, but I know that You have big things for me to do, so I pray that I always do Your works first. Amen.

Day 17

Pray For Your Family

Isaiah 11:6 .... And a little child shall lead them

One thing about being a kid is that you don't feel the weight on your shoulders like your parents do, so before we move forward, praise God for your childhood and that you are blessed to be a blessing to your family.

Did you know that being a military family means there are a lot of pressures that your family goes through that you don't see? One thing that God tells us to do is to pray for one another because sometimes others are going through things that we don't know about. Keep your family in prayer at all times so that you will not fall apart during tough times, but that you will grow in strength together. Pray for your family in both the good and bad times because there are times when you as the kid can pray harder than even your parents. Life will throw changes at you when you don't realize it, but praying for your family before things happen will position God in your family's life to bring you through it.

Prayer:

Lord, I pray for my family that You will strengthen us when we are weak and that we will see You show Yourself strong in our lives. Pour Your anointing upon us and keep us safe so that we will always find victory through You. Amen.

Day 18

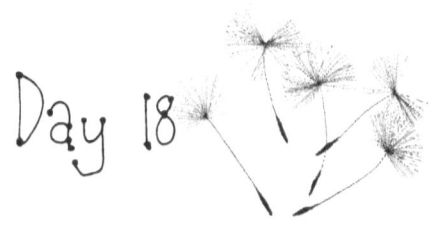

There Are Days That I Am Tired

Isaiah 40:29 The Lord gives strength to those who are tired. He gives more power to those who are weak.

There are going to be days when you feel that you have nothing left inside of you and all you want to do is quit and not keep moving. The thing about that though is that it's not an option.

We all have days where some are rougher than others, but we are not to quit because when times are the toughest is when God is gearing up to do the biggest thing in our lives. We just can't quit. When running a race, it is at the end when you are the most tired, but if you keep your eyes on the goal, you can finish the race! God does not want us to finish first, second, or last, but He wants us to *finish* the race. He wants to see that we will keep moving forward and seeking Him, no matter the cost. Pray for His strength when you feel the weakest and you will see that when you get to that goal after holding on the whole time that it will be all worth it. Get excited even when you're tired!

Prayer:

Lord, I pray that You give me supernatural strength to keep running the race of faith. I want to please You even when I am tired, so help me not to quit but to keep going. I want to endure to the end no matter what and see Your glory in the end. Amen.

Day 19

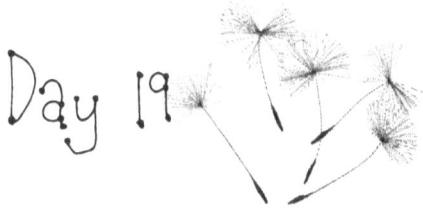

What New Adventures Will Lie Ahead?

Isaiah 43:18 & 19 The Lord says, "Forget what happened before. Do not think about the past. Look at the new thing I am going to do......"

New moves will always have new adventures to look forward to!

When you are told you are moving, what is the first thing you think about? I know that many kids start looking at what cool things are there to do at their next home. God gives us new adventures so that we can take a look at all the marvelous things He has created for us to see. Looking forward to new adventures can definitely make moving an exciting time because you will get to experience a whole new life in a new place. You might get to climb tall mountains, see old castles, walk in places that you only read about in books, or even get to build snowmen. Whatever adventure lies ahead of you, be excited and go full force to take it all in and not waste a single minute of that blessing.

Prayer:

Father, I ask that I get to experience as many adventures as I can. I want to see all of Your creations and I praise You that, as a military kid, I get this chance! Father God, the works of Your hands are beautiful, and I thank You for creating it just for me. Amen.

Day 20

I Am Who I Am Because God Made Me To Be Who I Am

Jeremiah 1:5 "Before I made you in your mother's womb, I chose you. Before you were born, I set you apart for a special work. I appointed you as a prophet to the nations."

Did you know there is only one you? There has never been, nor will there ever be, another one of you.

God knew you before you were ever formed in your mother's belly who you were going to be, and He also knew that He needed YOU as a military kid. He knew that you were going to be strong enough, brave enough, and smart enough to handle this military life. There might be days when you question who you are, but stop and remind yourself that you are a Child of the Most-High God and that you were set apart for this time to be in the position you are in. God is your creator and your father. Remind yourself that you are not a failure, but you are victorious because Christ lives in you!

Prayer:

Father God, I pray that I always remember what my purpose is that You have created me for and that I stand on Your truth when I can't seem to find my way. I want to fulfill my mission as a military kid and to help others stay strong. I thank You for my life because You made me perfect! Amen.

Day 21

With A New Place,

We Have The Opportunity For A New Ministry

2 Timothy 4:2 Preach the Good News. Be ready at all times...

As children of the Most-High God, we are to be His disciples that spread His good Word and, when we move, we have the opportunity to have a new ministry.

To have a ministry you don't have to have a church building or a bunch of people sitting and listening to you. In school, you can get some of your friends together and during lunch have a Bible study and prayer time. The ministry that God gives you is for a certain time of your life that fits where you are. God places us in certain places because He knows that we have a purpose there, and maybe someone you meet will need to have you as a friend and will need you to speak the Word of God to them. But you have to read your Bible so that you know the Word, so when someone asks you about the Bible, you know the Scriptures and can tell them the good news of Jesus!

Prayer:

Father, I pray that You use me in a mighty way in the place You have us right now and that I will think of Your Word all day. I choose to do Your will and I ask You to send me to speak to the right people and help me to lead others to You, no matter what. My relationship with You is my first responsibility and I take it seriously. Again, use me, Lord! Amen.

Day 22

You Are Worth So Much!

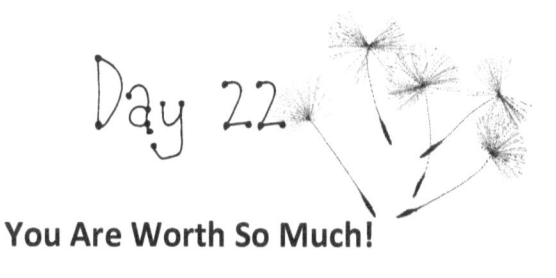

Psalm 139:14 I praise you because you made me in an amazing and wonderful way. What you have done is wonderful. I know this very well.

Did you know that God needs you? He needs you for so many things because you are a part of the body of Christ and without you, something doesn't fit.

There is not enough money in the entire world that could match your worth. God chose you out of so many people to help Him. The biggest thing that Jesus did for us that showed us what He thought of us was when He died on the cross for our sins. Jesus did that act because you are worth it all because He could not imagine Heaven without you. You are worth so much to your friends, family, church, school, and everything else you are involved in. Do not let mean words that are spoken or wrongful acts against you make you lose sight of your worth to Christ, and all those who love you. Remember to love yourself as well!

Prayer:

Lord, I thank You for my life and I thank You for dying on the cross for my sins because You saw my worth. If there comes a time when I feel like I am not worth anything, I pray You remind me anyway You can. Father, I thank You and I love You because You are worth more to me than anything else in this world! Amen!

Day 23

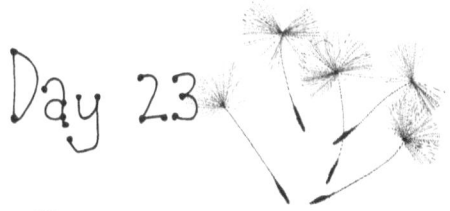

Keep The Military In Your Prayers

Isaiah 6:8 Then I heard the Lord's voice. He said, "Whom can I send? Who will go for us?" So I said, "Here I am. Send me!"

One thing about those who are in the military is that they were not told they had to go in the military, but they chose to serve our country.

Being a military member has to be a tough decision since there are so many things that are expected of them. They are the ones that have to leave their families, go to dangerous places, and go to school for pretty much the whole time. They carry a lot of weight for the decision they make to help keep our country safe. Maybe you can't go with your mom or dad when the military calls them away, but one thing you can do is to pray for them. Pray for them before they leave, while they are gone, and even when they are at home. Pray for the military as a group as well because there might be some members that do not have someone to pray for them, and they need all the prayers they can get. Keep praying for them, God is hearing you!

Prayer:

Lord, in my time of prayer I want to set aside my prayers for myself and pray for those who have answered the call to serve our country. I pray that You cover them with Your protection and that You heal them if they are hurt. Keep watch over those members and their families while they are apart. Thank You, Lord, for our military members. Amen.

Day 24

Our Friends Need Prayers

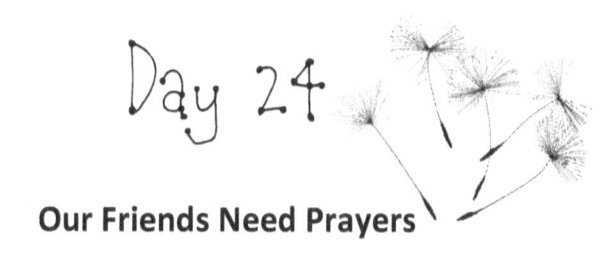

1 Thessalonians 5:17 Never stop praying…

There is not one person in this world that does not need prayer and one group of people that you know very well is no exception.

Our friends are those that are the closest to us, and those who we share secrets with that we know will keep it to themselves. But what happens when a friend tells you about something that is bothering them? Instantly, right then and there, pray for them. Don't wait to pray for your friends, especially if they tell you something that could use prayer. If they are nervous, scared, or sad because their mom or dad is gone, whatever the case may be, just pray. Your friends just knowing that someone is praying for them can give them peace and comfort that they did not have before. No prayer goes unheard when you are praying to the Almighty God, because He cares for ours and our friends' burdens.

Prayer:

Lord, I pray for my friends that I know have needs and for those who I don't know have needs. You know, Lord, who needs what, so I pray that you go and reveal Yourself to my friends and fix what they need work in. Amen.

Day 25

Create Forever Memories

Philippians 4:8 Brothers, continue to think about the things that are good and worthy of praise. Think about the things that are true and honorable and right and pure and beautiful and respected.

Moving to different places gives way to making lasting memories that you will carry with you through your life.

As you begin to explore your new home, make sure that you are present in the moment. It is ok to have a phone to take pictures but be careful to take in the scenery in real-time too. When you are on a beach, make sandcastles, bury your family members in the sand, and possibly look for seashells. This way, when you grow up, or your family member that is in the military has to leave you can make a project to remember those times with. Memories are those things that you can carry with you and they never get destroyed. God gives us memories, so in the times that we are not happy, we can think about the wonderful things we have been able to do, which makes our heart feel better as well.

Prayer:

Father, I pray that I create memories that I will be able to carry with me forever. As I enjoy my time with my family and in those special places, help my brain to store it all in. I am so grateful to You, Father God, for giving me these special times to create memories. Amen.

Day 26

Mom And Dad Need Your Help

Colossians 3:20 Children, obey your parents in all things. This pleases the Lord.

One of the things God asks us to do is to obey our parents and not just because they are older than you but because respect goes a long way.

When you obey your parents, you are gaining their trust, knowing that they can rely on you for help. When your parent is gone for a long time or not, obeying your parents is a must because God commands you to do it. If your parent is gone then, sometimes, the parent that is home needs a little more help, so instead of waiting for them to tell you what they want you to do, why not ask them how you can help. This communication is the same as it is with our communication with God. Instead of always asking God for something, why not ask

Him what you can do for Him. Your obedience with your parents should reflect your relationship with God since He is our Heavenly Father. So, go ahead, and put the book down and ask your parents what they need help with.

Prayer:

Father, I want to first thank You for my parents and how hard they work to give me what I need. I want to be a blessing to them as they are to me. Help me to be patient and understanding of what is needed and where I can help a little more. Amen.

Day 27

I Am Proud To Be A Military Kid!

Colossians 3:17 Everything you say and everything you do should all be done for Jesus your Lord. And in all you do, give thanks to God the Father through Jesus.

Being a military kid is a privilege!

To be a military kid you have to be tough, strong, brave, and ready for anything, but the greatest part about being a military kid is that you can be proud of your position. You get to stand with other military kids that have had to say 'goodbye' and move more than once, all while supporting your parent, who is in the military. God tells us to do everything for Jesus and that goes for being a military kid. When you tell people that you are a military kid and they say, "I don't know how you do it!" tell them, "It's because of God's strength I can stand strong!" Sometimes, the military kid life is not fair, but you are in a group of some extraordinary kids, who have extraordinary strength to endure the long days and months of waiting for someone to return or to start a new life. Don't shy away from your position as a military kid, but be proud of who you are and what you get to do!

Prayer:

Lord, I pray that I always stay proud of the position You have put me in as a military kid and that on those tough days that I just can't find the strength to keep on, I know You are on my side lifting me up. I love being part of the military family as a military kid and I want to do everything for Your glory. Amen.

Day 28

Be Proud of Your Parents

Exodus 20:12 Honor your father and your mother. Then you will live a long time in the land. The Lord your God is going to give you this land.

When you grow up and have kids you will see how hard your parents work to make sure you stay healthy and fed.

God wants us to honor our parents and one way to do that is to be proud of your parent no matter what. Being a military member makes them stay away from home for long periods of time. Be proud of that parent answering that call to serve. If you have a parent that stays home and does not work, be proud of that parent because that isn't an easy job either. God called your parents to do certain things in this season of their lives, so don't look down on them, but be proud of them! Let them know you're proud and thankful for them. Also pray for your parents because they need your prayers, too.

Prayer:

Lord, I thank You for parents that are hardworking, loving, protective, and obedient to You. I am blessed to be the child of the greatest parents around and I want to do all I can to honor them, so bless my parents. I pray that You give my parents the desires of their hearts and that I can be like them one day. Amen.

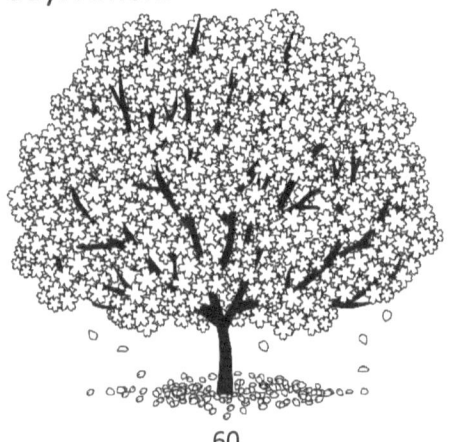

Day 29

Creating Your World

Jeremiah 29:11 I say this because I know what I have planned for you," says the Lord. "I have good plans for you. I don't plan to hurt you. I plan to give you hope and a good future."

Did you know that you can change the world that you live in?

It might seem like a big task to change the world, but by just doing your part, no matter how small, can have a domino effect on others. Imagine that you don't like hearing someone bully a friend of yours. Do you sit back and watch, or do you get up and support your friend? God has big plans for you, and He does not want us sitting back and doing nothing. He wants us to help those who are hurting. If you see that there is something wrong, then pray that the Lord will give you a strategy to make a change that will have a good impact. When it is time to leave your school because of a move, you want people to remember you for the good things, which comes with creating your world in a positive way. You don't have to go along with the crowd when people pressure you, but you can create your own crowd of people who want to obey and have peace like you.

Prayer:

Father, You created this world that we live in and I want to create the world I live in with the help of Your loving spirit. I choose to not be a part of the things this world wants me to do but I choose to create a world that wants more of You! Thank You for Your plans for my life! Amen.

Day 30

Grow Where You're Planted

Jeremiah 17:7 & 8 "But the person who trusts in the Lord will be blessed. The Lord will show him that he can be trusted. He will be strong, like a tree planted near water. That tree has large roots that find the water. It is not afraid when the days are hot. Its leaves are always green. It does not worry in a year when no rain comes. That tree always produces fruit."

Wow, isn't it amazing how when God puts you somewhere that He gives you everything you need to thrive there!?!

Wherever God moves you to, always know that He has a plan and a purpose for you to be right where you are at that moment. He will connect you with people who will bless you and encourage you if you just trust Him. At first, it may seem like you will never grow there but keep your hands in God's hands and He will keep your feet steady. As you stay there and pray, you will see that you will start to grow stronger and bigger than when you first got to your new home. One thing that you have to do is allow God to water you and shine His light on you so that in your new place you will be planted, and no one can take you out. God will take care of all your needs to grow where He has planted you, but make sure to be thankful for all that He has done for you!

Prayer:

Father God, how awesome You are for not just the things You have done for me, but through me. I pray that You show me new opportunities that I can involve myself in that will make me grow in the areas I don't know. You are my Creator and I know that You take care of me and I cannot wait to see what lies ahead of me and where I will grow. Amen!

Prayer Requests For Me

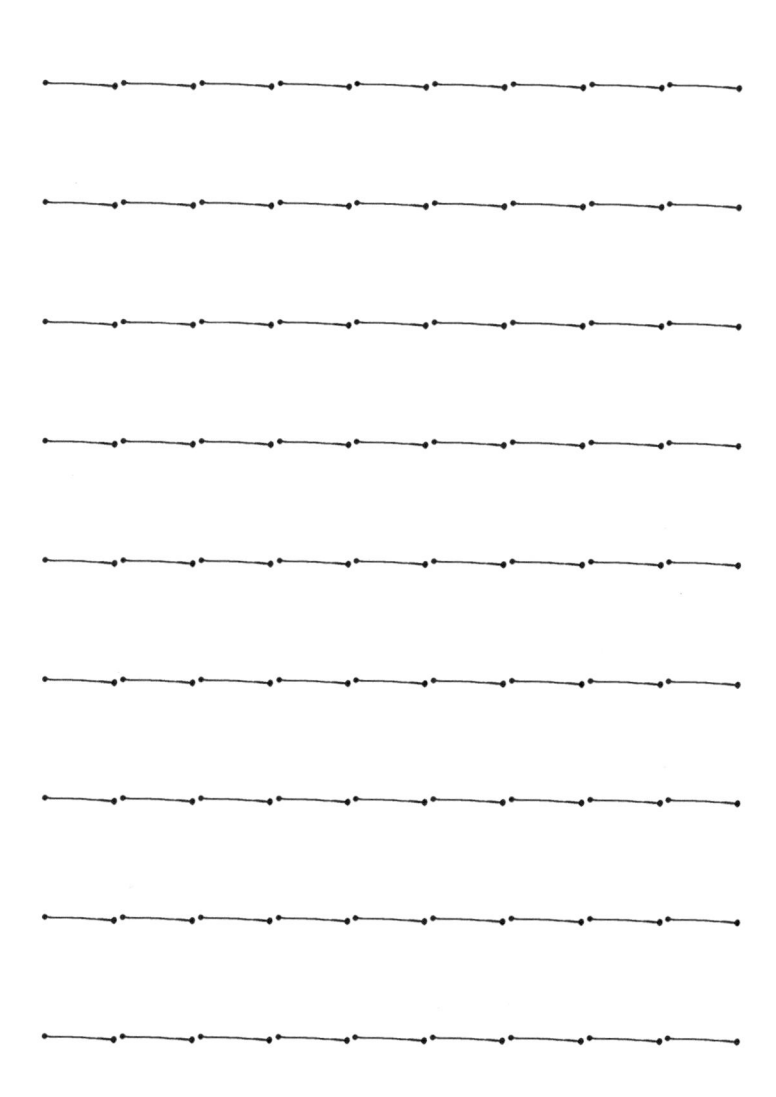

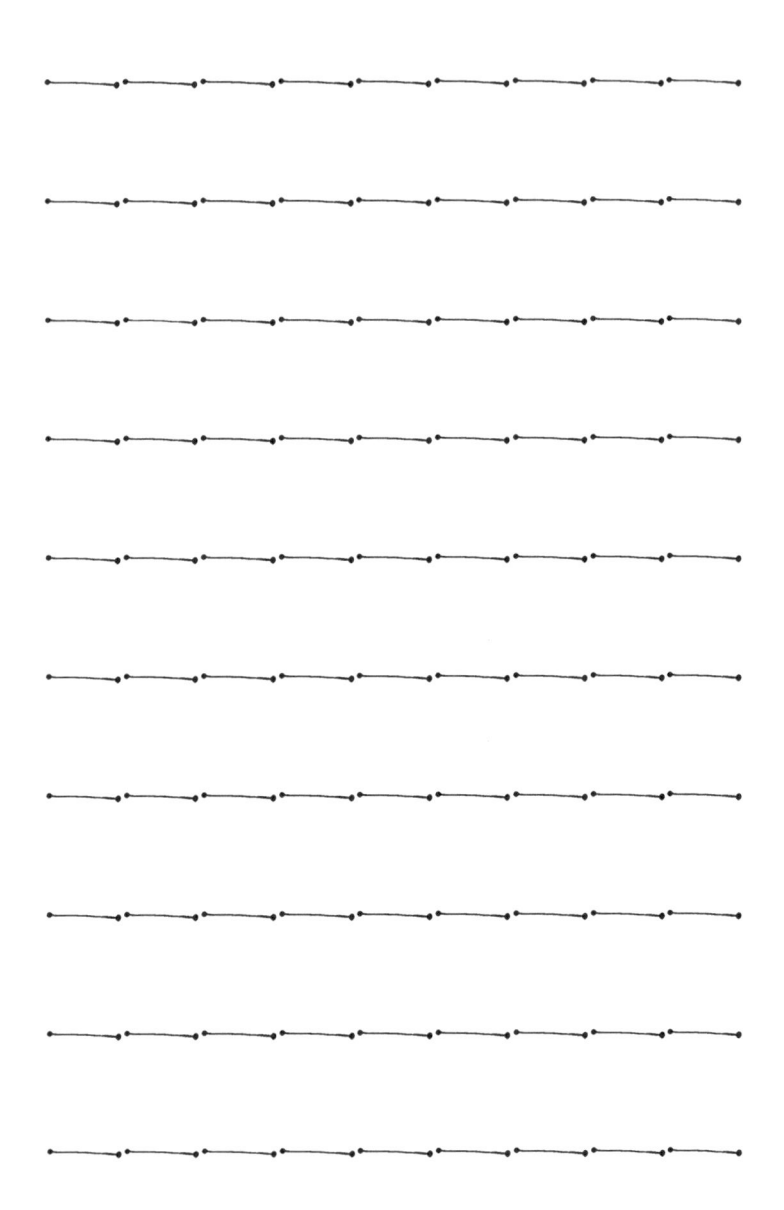

Prayer Requests For My Friends

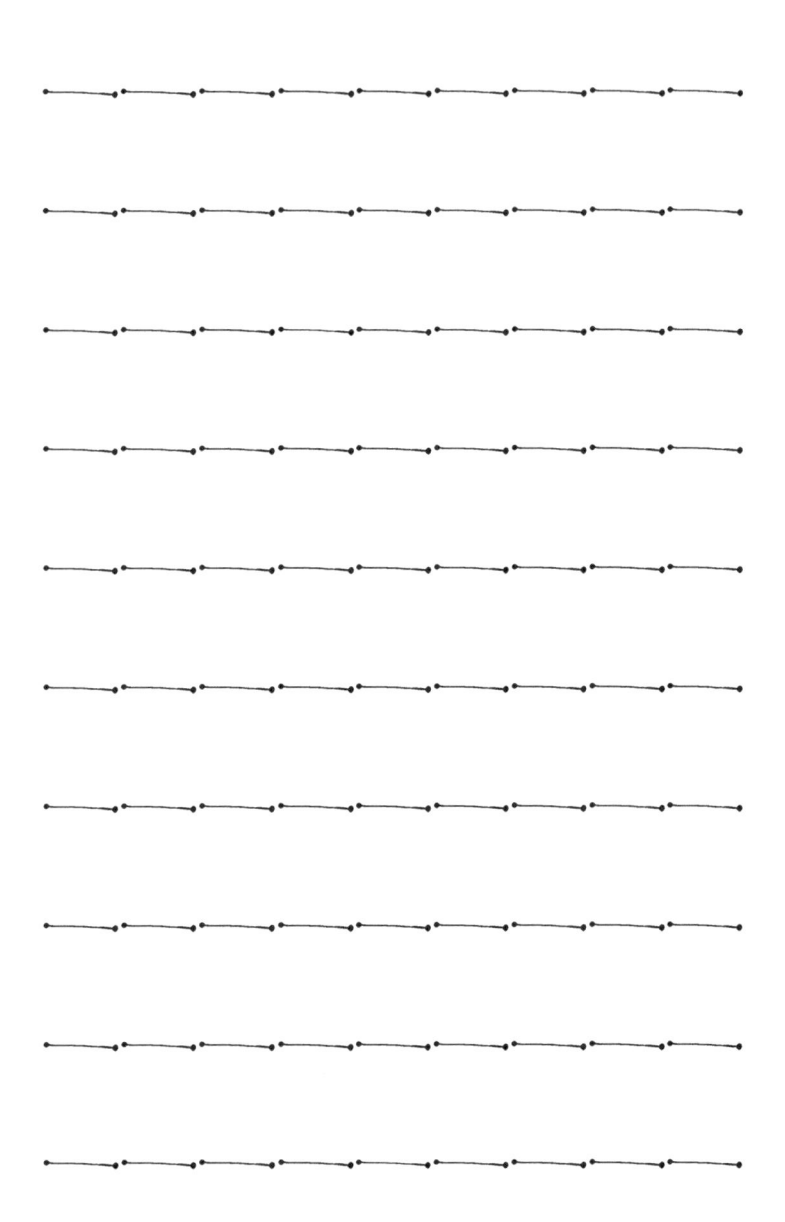

Places I Have Lived & What I Love About Them

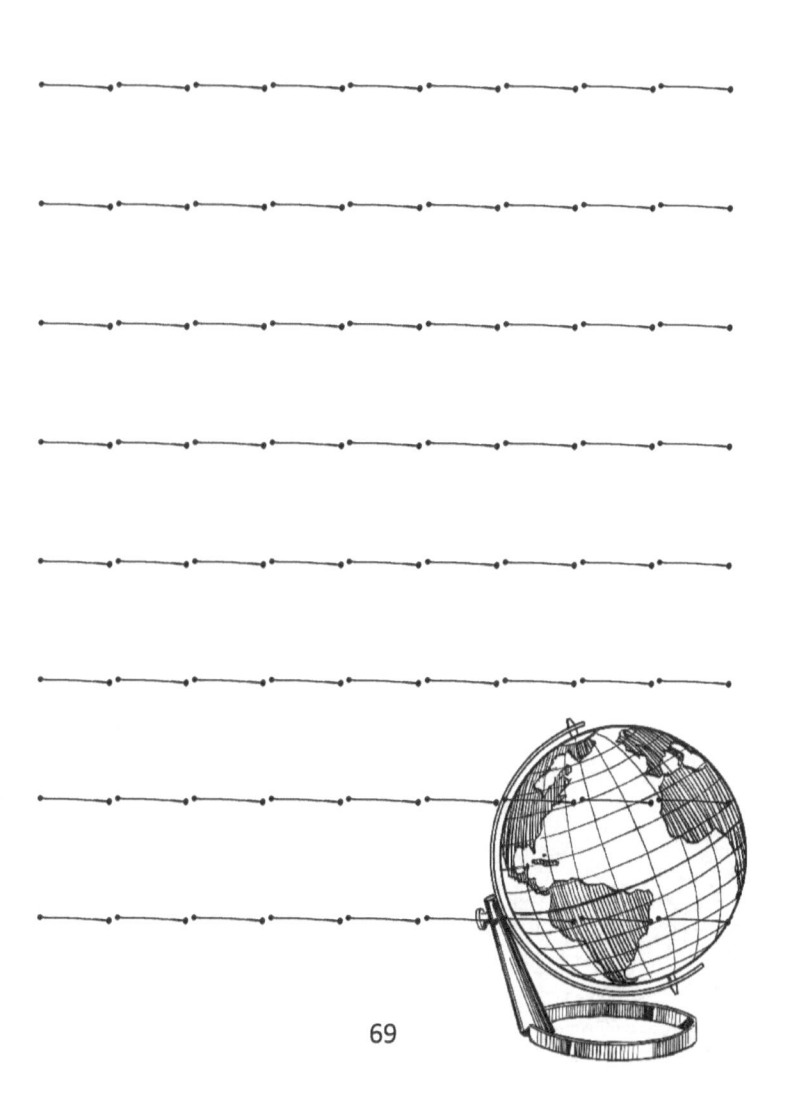

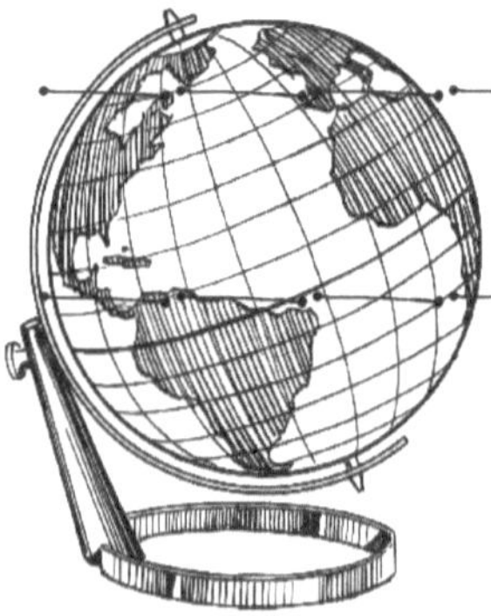

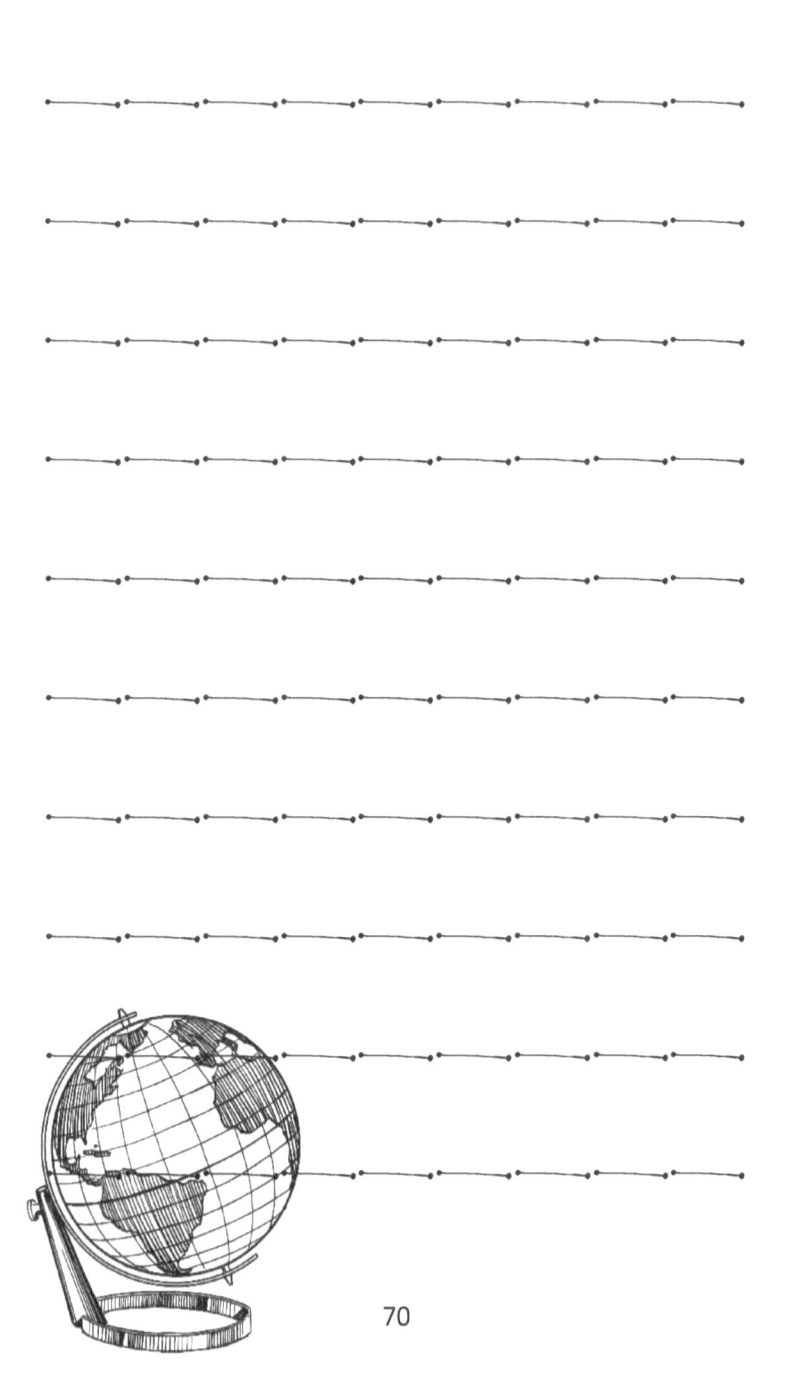

Friends & Family Contacts

Name: _____

Phone: _____

Address: _____

Name: _____

Phone: _____

Address: _____

Name: _____

Phone: _____

Address: _____

Name: _____

Phone:_____

Address:_____

Name: _____

Phone:_____

Address:_____

Name: _____

Phone:_____

Address:_____

Name: _____

Phone:_____

Address:_____

Name: _____

Phone:_____

Address:_____

Name: _____

Phone:_____

Address:_____

Name: _____

Phone:_____

Address:_____

Name: _____

Phone:_____

Address:_____

Name: _____

Phone:_____

Address:_____

Name: _____

Phone: _____

Address: _____

Name: _____

Phone: _____

Address: _____

Name: _____

Phone: _____

Address: _____

Name: _____

Phone:_____

Address:_____

Name: _____

Phone:_____

Address:_____

Name: _____

Phone:_____

Address:_____

Thank You!

I want to thank you from the bottom of my heart for purchasing this devotional for you and your family to study. These devotions come from my time of raising my children in the military world, seeking God for guidance, and applying the Word to situations that come up. My prayer for you is that no matter where God takes you that you will be abundantly blessed beyond measure. God's Word promises us in Eph 3:20 (ICB) - *With God's power working in us, God can do much, much more than anything we can ask or think of.*

If you would, after reading and studying this devotional, please leave a review on Amazon to help share about this devotional with other military families.

You can also reach me with any comments at:
laura.patton1@yahoo.com

Made in United States
Troutdale, OR
04/16/2025

30662573R00046